Text Structures

Big Cats
Head to Head

A Compare and Contrast Text

Phillip Simpson

Chicago, Illinois

© 2015 Heinemann Library
an imprint of Capstone Global Library, LLC
Chicago, Illinois

All rights reserved. No part of this publication may be reproduced or transmitted in any form or by any means, electronic or mechanical, including photocopying, recording, taping, or any information storage and retrieval system, without permission in writing from the publisher.

Edited by Diyan Leake and Kathryn Clay
Designed by Steve Mead
Picture research by Tracy Cummins
Production by Helen McCreath
Originated by Capstone Global Library Ltd
Printed and bound in China by Leo Paper Group

18 17 16
10 9 8 7 6 5 4 3 2

Library of Congress Cataloging-in-Publication Data
Simpson, Phillip W., 1971-
Big cats head to head : a compare and contrast text / Phillip Simpson.
    pages cm.—(Text structures)
Includes bibliographical references and index.
ISBN 978-1-4846-0414-4 (pb)
1. Panthera—Juvenile literature. I. Title.
QL737.C23S5615 2015
599.75'5—dc23   2013040368

Photo Credits
Corbis: Ch'ien Lee, 5 top middle; Getty Images: Dhammika Heenpella/Images of Sri Lanka, 26, Manoj Shah, 27, Ryan McVay, 10; Naturepl.com: © Andy Rouse, 6, 17, 20, 22, © Anup Shah, 4 right, 18, 21, © Ashok Jain, 9, © E.A. KUTTAPAN, 14, © Edwin Giesbers, 12, © LYNN M. STONE, 5 top right, 13; Shutterstock: andamanec, 5 bottom middle, Anna Omelchenko, 5 left, apiguide, front cover, Colette3, 4 middle, Deborah Kolb, front cover, Dennis Donohue, 24, e2dan, 11, Eduard Kyslynskyy, 15 right, Jakub Krechowicz, 29 (notebook), Mogens Trolle, 19 right, Ohishiapply, 28, Pal Teravagimov, 4 top left, Pearl Media, 4 bottom left, 19 left, Phillipa Pieterse, 15 left, S.R. Maglione, 16, Sarah Cheriton-Jones, 5 bottom right, urfin, 29 (pen), Volodymyr Burdiak, 23, worldswildlifewonders, 15 middle; SuperStock: Belinda Images, 25

Artistic Effects
Shutterstock: Livijus Raubickas, nico99, Olga Kovalenko, Peshkova, Roman Sotola

Every effort has been made to contact copyright holders of material reproduced in this book. Any omissions will be rectified in subsequent printings if notice is given to the publisher.

All the Internet addresses (URLs) given in this book were valid at the time of going to press. However, due to the dynamic nature of the Internet, some addresses may have changed, or sites may have changed or ceased to exist since publication. While the author and publisher regret any inconvenience this may cause readers, no responsibility for any such changes can be accepted by either the author or the publisher.

Contents

Big Cats 4
What is a Big Cat? 6
Where Big Cats Live 8
Roaring 10
Body Size 12
Fur 14
Speed 16
Skull Size 18
Hunting 20
Habitat 22
Diet 24
Social Skills 26
Explanation of Text Structure 28
Glossary 30
Find Out More 31
Index 32

The text in this book has been organized using the compare and contrast text structure. Comparing and contrasting shows how things are similar and how they are different. To find out more about writing using this text structure, see page 28.

Some words are shown in bold, **like this**. You can find out what they mean by looking in the glossary.

Big Cats

The term "big cats" is used to refer to large cats found in the wild. All big cats are **mammals** and **carnivores**. The true big cats are tigers, lions, jaguars, and leopards. These are the only big cats that can roar. They have many **characteristics** in common.

> Jaguars, lions, tigers, and leopards are considered to be true big cats because they can roar.

The snow leopard, clouded leopard, and the Sunda clouded leopard are also considered big cats. Cheetahs and pumas are often classified as big cats, even though they are not as closely related.

Cheetahs, Sunda clouded leopards, snow leopards, clouded leopards, and pumas are also big cats.

What is a Big Cat?

The **classification** of a big cat can be confusing because some small cats are actually quite big. And some big cats are quite small. A cat's eyes can help to tell what kind of cat it is. In daylight big cats have round pupils, while small cats have pupils like slits. Clouded and Sunda clouded leopards have oblong-shaped pupils all the time.

Tigers have round pupils in daylight.

With the exception of snow leopards, big cats generally eat lying down rather than crouched over their food. Tigers, lions, leopards, and jaguars are able to roar because of their throat structure. However, even though cheetahs, clouded leopards, Sunda clouded leopards, snow leopards, and pumas are considered big cats, they cannot roar.

Big cat	Roars	Round pupils in daylight	Large size	Eats lying down
Tiger	Yes	Yes	Yes	Yes
Lion	Yes	Yes	Yes	Yes
Jaguar	Yes	Yes	Yes	Yes
Leopard	Yes	Yes	Yes	Yes
Cheetah	No	Yes	Yes	Yes
Puma	No	Yes	Yes	Yes
Snow leopard	No	Yes	Yes	No
Clouded leopard	No	No	No	Yes
Sunda clouded leopard	No	No	No	Yes

Where Big Cats Live

Big cats are found all over the world. Cheetahs, leopards, and lions are most commonly found in Africa. Sunda clouded leopards, clouded leopards, snow leopards, and tigers are found in Asian countries such as India and Russia. Pumas and jaguars live in North and South America.

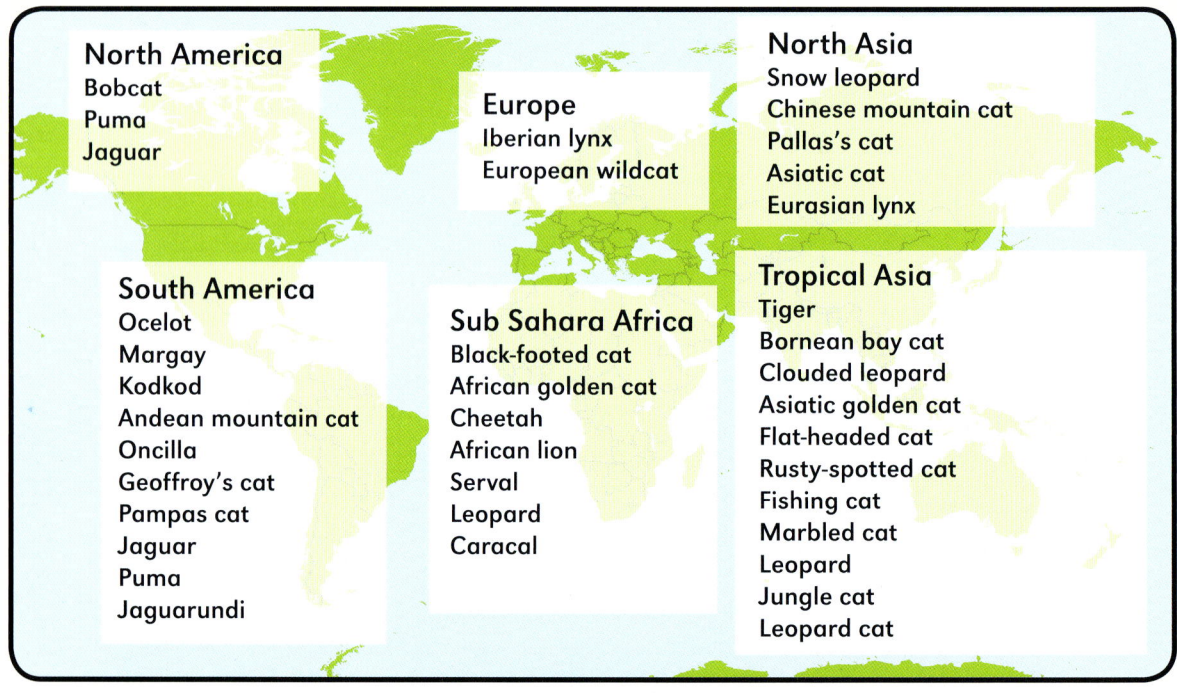

North America
Bobcat
Puma
Jaguar

Europe
Iberian lynx
European wildcat

North Asia
Snow leopard
Chinese mountain cat
Pallas's cat
Asiatic cat
Eurasian lynx

South America
Ocelot
Margay
Kodkod
Andean mountain cat
Oncilla
Geoffroy's cat
Pampas cat
Jaguar
Puma
Jaguarundi

Sub Sahara Africa
Black-footed cat
African golden cat
Cheetah
African lion
Serval
Leopard
Caracal

Tropical Asia
Tiger
Bornean bay cat
Clouded leopard
Asiatic golden cat
Flat-headed cat
Rusty-spotted cat
Fishing cat
Marbled cat
Leopard
Jungle cat
Leopard cat

This map shows where big cats live.

Big cats live in a wide range of **habitats**, from open savannahs to rain forests and even snow-topped mountains. In recent years destruction of their habitats has resulted in their numbers falling.

The clearing of forests leaves less room for big cats to live and hunt.

Roaring

Tigers, lions, jaguars, and leopards can roar because part of their throat, known as the larynx, is different from that of other cats. Their larynxes are longer so that when air passes through, the walls of the larynx vibrate and create sound.

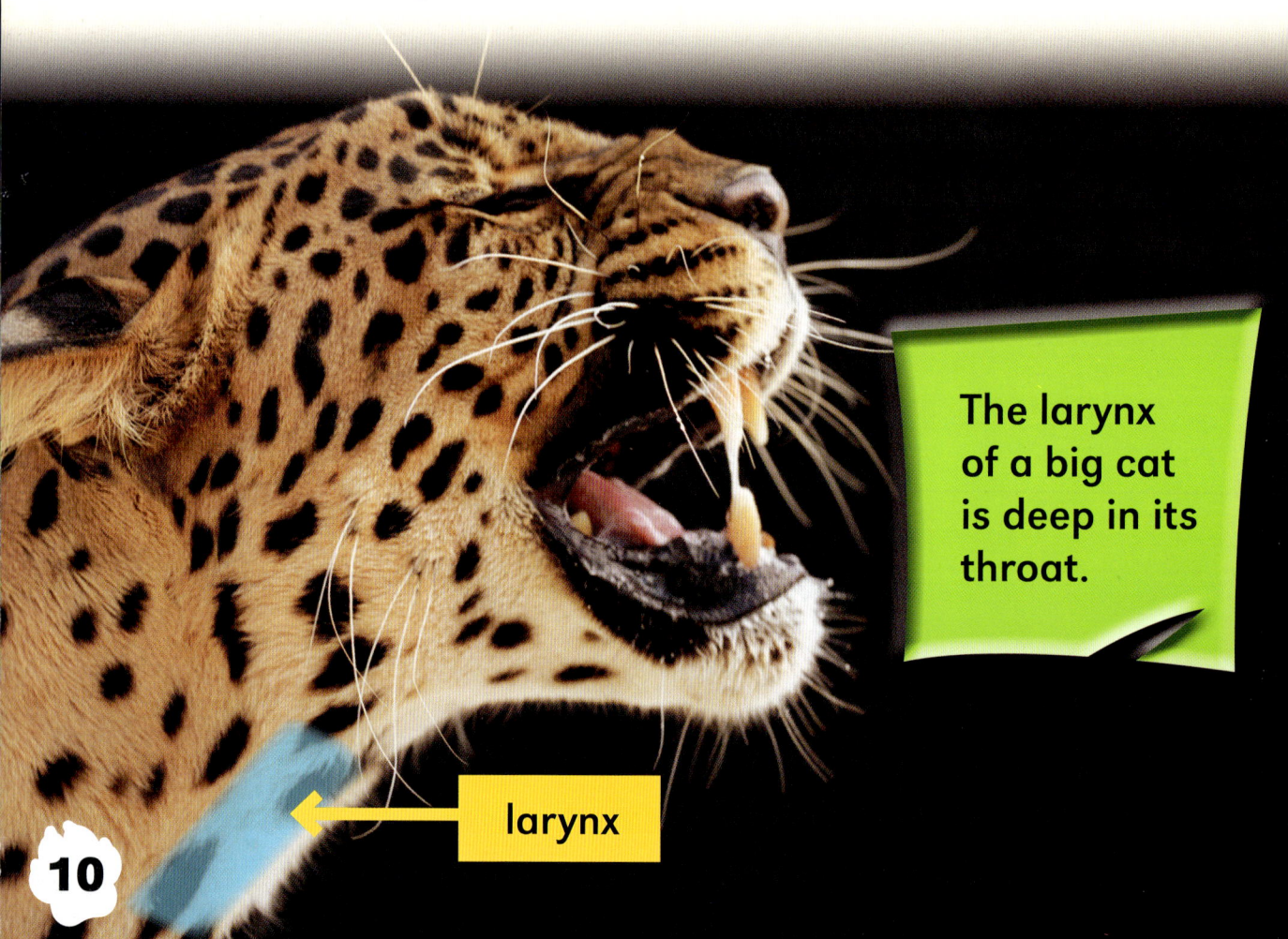

The larynx of a big cat is deep in its throat.

larynx

Lions have the largest larynx of any big cat. This gives them the loudest roar.

Cats roar for many reasons, though mainly to warn intruders to stay away. They also roar to call to their young and to find mates. The lion has the loudest roar of all the big cats. It can be heard from up to 5 miles (8 kilometers) away. Like the lion, the tiger also has a powerful roar. But a tiger's roar can only be heard from 1.8 miles (2.9 kilometers) away.

Body Size

Big cats are extremely varied when it comes to size. The tiger is the largest of the big cats, and the Siberian tiger is the largest of this species. It has a body length of 75 to 90 inches (190 to 229 centimeters), with a tail measuring 24 to 43 inches (61 to 109 centimeters). A male Siberian tiger can weigh more than 661 pounds (300 kilograms).

The Siberian tiger is the largest of the big cats.

The snow leopard weighs 77 to 121 pounds (35 to 55 kilograms).

The smallest of the big cats are snow leopards and cheetahs. The snow leopard is only 47 to 59 inches (119 to 150 centimeters) long, with a tail of about 35 inches (89 centimeters). The cheetah is a similar size, but it has a shorter tail of 26 to 31 inches (66 to 79 centimeters).

Fur

All big cats **stalk** their **prey**. To do this, they must blend in with their surroundings, making it difficult for their prey to spot them. Each species of big cat has fur that acts as **camouflage**. The fur color and type depends on the habitat in which the big cat is found.

A leopard's black spots help it to blend in with its surroundings.

The spots of cheetahs, jaguars, and leopards are all different.

The tiger has stripes, while the lion has plain tan fur. The snow leopard, the leopard, and the jaguar all have black spots on their fur. The leopard has a flower-like pattern of black spots known as rosettes. The jaguar's fur is similar, but its rosettes have a black dot inside. The snow leopard has both black spots and rosettes.

Speed

For most of the big cats, running fast is necessary for hunting and catching prey. However, big cats can only move fast for a short time. If a chase goes on too long, the prey animals usually get away because they can run for longer periods.

> It takes tigers many attempts to catch prey. Only about 1 in 10 hunts is successful.

Cheetahs are the only big cats that cannot fully retract, or pull in, their claws. They need them out to stay stable when running.

The cheetah is the fastest land mammal on Earth. It can reach speeds of about 70 miles (113 kilometers) per hour. Female lions can reach speeds of 50 miles (80 kilometers) per hour.

Skull Size

The size of a big cat's skull gives an idea of what size prey it can kill. Cats with larger skulls are able to hunt larger prey. A big skull usually means a big jaw. A big cat with a larger jaw is able to bite the throat of a larger prey animal.

A big cat usually chokes its prey.

Lions and tigers have much larger skulls than other big cats.

Lions and tigers have the biggest skulls of all the big cats. They also hunt the biggest prey, such as buffalo and large antelope. Leopards and jaguars have similar-sized skulls, while cheetahs, pumas, and snow leopards have much smaller skulls.

Hunting

Most big cats are nocturnal. This means they hunt at night. Many prey animals are less active or even asleep at night. This makes it easier for big cats to stalk and kill them. Big cats are also much harder to spot in the dark.

Hunting at night helps big cats stay hidden from their prey.

Cheetahs are most active during the day.

Unlike other big cats, jaguars and snow leopards usually hunt at dawn or dusk. This behavior is known as crepuscular. In contrast, cheetahs are diurnal, which means they mostly hunt during the day.

Habitat

Big cats are found in the same habitats as their prey animals. Big cats have also adapted, or changed, to fit in with their habitats. Their bodies, hunting techniques, fur, jaws, and claws all enable them to hunt and live in a certain type of habitat.

A lion's fur color closely matches the savannah.

Siberian tigers have thick coats of fur to help them stay warm in snow-covered habitats.

The open grassland of Africa is known as the savannah. Lions, leopards, and cheetahs live there. The jaguar's habitat is the tropical rain forest, while the Siberian tiger prefers snow-covered forests. Pumas also live in forests, but their habitat includes mountain regions. Snow leopards, like pumas, live in mountain regions that are often covered in snow.

Diet

All big cats are carnivores that hunt and kill prey animals. A bigger cat can generally hunt and kill bigger prey. Some big cats are also scavengers. This means that they will eat a dead animal that they did not kill.

Lions hunt in groups and share their food.

Tigers and lions hunt the biggest prey, but even they will not usually take on huge animals such as elephants. A snow leopard can sometimes kill prey three times its size. The cheetah eats smaller prey such as gazelles and impalas. The jaguar's powerful bite enables it to eat turtles and other reptiles.

A cheetah's speed helps it catch prey.

Social Skills

Most big cats are solitary hunters and live alone. They are territorial, which means they guard the area they live in. They will generally fight off other members of their own species. However, during the mating season, the male and female of the species stay together long enough for the female to become pregnant.

Adult leopards will only spend time together during mating season.

An elephant chases away a lion pride.

Only a few big cats live in groups. Lions are very **social** animals. They live in groups known as prides and work together during hunts. Cheetah males sometimes hunt and live together in groups of two or three.

Explanation of Text Structure

This text focuses on comparing and contrasting. When you **compare and contrast** two or more things, you examine ways in which they are alike or different. Words that tell you something is being compared or contrasted include: *like, unlike, different, similar, both, also, although, but, more, while, even though, in common, in contrast, compared with,* and *however.*

Leopards and jaguars have similar-sized skulls. **Unlike** other big cats, lions are social animals. The jaguar's habitat is the tropical rainforest, **while** the Siberian tiger prefers snow-covered forests that are drier. **Like** the lion, the tiger **also** has a powerful roar.

Compare and contrast signal words

> Now you could try using the **compare and contrast** text structure to write about:
> - your school and a school in a different country
> - a butterfly and a moth
> - a burrow and a nest

Glossary

camouflage a natural coloring or body shape that allows an animal to blend in with its surroundings

carnivore an animal that eats meat

characteristic a feature or quality of an animal or place that helps to identify it

classification an arrangement of animals and plants into groups according to their similarities

habitat a natural home for an animal or plant

mammal an animal that has hair on its body and feeds its babies with milk from the mother

prey an animal that is hunted and eaten by other animals

social preferring to live in groups

stalk to follow silently and slowly

Find out more

Books
Bloom, Steve. *Big Cats: In Search of Lions, Leopards, Cheetahs, and Tigers.* New York: Thames and Hudson, 2012.

Carney, Elizabeth. *Everything Big Cats.* Washington, D.C.: National Geographic, 2011.

Dale, Jay. *Top Ten Big Cats.* Mankato, Minn.: Smart Apple Media, 2012.

Websites
www.bbc.co.uk/nature/life/Felidae
Find out more about the cat family on this website.

gowild.wwf.org.uk/regions/americas-fact-files/jaguar
Check out the World Wildlife Fund's fact file about the jaguar.

Index

Africa, 8, 23
Asia, 8

body size, 12, 13

carnivores, 4, 24
cheetahs, 5, 7, 8, 13, 17, 19, 21, 23, 25, 27
clouded leopards, 5, 6, 7, 8

eating, 7, 24
eyes, 6

fur, 14, 15, 22

habitats, 22, 23
hunting, 20, 21

India, 8

jaguars, 4, 7, 8, 10, 15, 19, 21, 23, 25

larynx, 10
leopards, 4, 7, 8, 10, 13, 14, 15, 19, 21, 23

lions, 4, 7, 8, 10, 11, 15, 17, 19, 23, 24, 25, 27

mating, 26

North America, 8

prey, 14, 16, 18, 19, 20, 22, 24, 25
pumas, 5, 7, 8, 19, 23

rain forests, 9, 23
roaring, 4, 7, 10, 11
Russia, 8

savannahs, 9, 23
skull, size of, 18, 19
snow leopards, 5, 6, 7, 8, 13, 15, 19, 21, 23, 25
South America, 8
Sunda clouded leopards, 5, 6, 7, 8

tigers, 4, 7, 8, 10, 11, 12, 15, 16, 19, 23, 25
  Siberian tigers, 12, 23